God, Grace, & Mercy

"Surviving Tough Times & Seasons of Marriage"

NATALIE WOOD RICHÉ

RicheContentCreations.com

Foreword

Life can really be defined by a series of providential relationships. The Bible is a book of Community; more specifically, God's active presence in the communal context of the Nation of Israel. As much as God wanted the nation's love and devotion; God equally wanted them to honor the blessing of being connected together in relationships that were mutually meaningful and spiritually necessary.

If anyone is blessed to guide us in a discussion of stewarding relationships and more specifically marital relationships, it's Natalie. I met her as an energetic and curious child and watched her grow to become an anointed and focused adult. Her life has been stewarding relationships on a large scale as she matured in the context of the Black Church her father pastors. Her young marriage and the addition of children to her family have stretched her in ways that have extracted the best of her gifts. Anyone needing guidance and encouragement in marital relationships, parenting and spiritual maturity, should read this book. It will bless your life and your marriage immensely.

Life can be defined by a series of providential relationships. My life has been blessed by meeting Natalie and yours will too. Be Blessed.

Dr. William H. Curtis

Senior Pastor

Mount Ararat Baptist Church

Contents

I wrote this book for couples to have rich, meaningful, and thought-provoking conversations. This book is a testament to the experiences I have encountered in my marriage. It is my prayer that you hear God's voice through the pages. My hope is this book helps others make it through tough times and seasons in their marriage. I dedicate this book to couples who desire to restore and rebuild their marriages from the ground up!

WELCOME & INTRODUCTION

As a daughter, sister, friend, wife, mother, and overall relationship enthusiast, I have always been intrigued by interpersonal relationships. Anyone who knows me will more than likely recall meaningful conversations around relationships and matters of the heart. Whether it's a girl's night or pillow talk with my husband, I long for a deeper understanding of relationships and how they frame people's worlds. As I researched marriage statistics, I discovered that divorce rates are at an all-time low. I rejoiced because the rates had declined, but the reality of the numbers was still staggering. Every 13 seconds, a divorce occurs, equating to around 300 divorces per hour, 7,000 divorces per day, 50,000 divorces per week, and two and a half million divorce cases per year.

Ten percent of failed marriages happen within the first two years and 20 percent within the first five years. That means one in ten couples will not survive the first two years of marriage, and 1 in 5 will not make it to year 5. It didn't take long for me to understand the depth of why these numbers are the way they are.

I knew all too well the struggle of marriage and how fragile it can be in the beginning. So many couples become a casualty of war in marriage. It made sense to me why some never made it past the first two stages of marriage. I believe I would have been among this statistical group of failed marriages if I didn't fast, pray, have Christian mentors, and sound advice. God, grace, and mercy were the three-strand cord that held my marriage together for me. This cord helped me hold on in times of struggle and kept me from calling it quits in my marriage.

Even through difficulties, I believe God, Grace, and Mercy are essential for successful marriages! Without these three qualities working within marriage, it becomes uncertain how to move forward with a spouse. The question then becomes, are you and your spouse both willing to embody these virtuous qualities and go through the process of becoming one?

GETTING TO KNOW YOU

Marriage is still one of the celebrated milestones in a person's life. It is usually an elaborately planned day that requires time and a lot of preparation. Traditionally, weddings are an event where families come together and celebrate the occasion. There is a sense of pride, respect, and reverence for the two who stand at the altar. In most cases, the party begins at the wedding reception!

The ceremonial part becomes a footnote, and then food, fun, and dancing become the focal point. As the time to eat, drink, dance, and be merry commences-there is a time set aside for speeches given by those closest to the bride and groom.

Often, these speeches reflect on past experiences, funny stories, and many well wishes to the couple as they set the trajectory of their new normal as a couple. Those guests who attend add to the celebration with gifts, gadgets, monetary donations, cards, and prayers for a prosperous marital journey.

Getting to know you:
On what day did you and your spouse get married?

What do you remember about that day?

What advice, if any, do you remember receiving on the wedding day that you have not forgotten?

Even with the outpouring of support, many do not make it till death do us part. I often wondered why? As I have embarked on my marital journey, I believe it is for a reason. It is the Amen of marriage, the apex of a vow fulfilled. Many couples live for the moment, not the journey. Who could blame them? They just decided to spend the rest of their life with the one person that makes them the happiest. However, the real test comes when the celebration fades, and everyone retreats to their respective places.

The beginning of their journey together starts. The metaphorical rubber meets the road, and there's no more time for timeouts or breaks! The two are now operating inside of a legal and spiritual binding agreement. Within these spiritual confines, couples find strength and power.

Discussion Question
Did you allow God to have any input in the spouse you chose?

There have long been debates about whether God honors marriages based upon His will or our desire. If you attended a church regularly as I did, the "unequally yoked" message was more than likely taught to you when choosing the right spouse. I think it makes for a great discussion, but I believe, no matter the choice, God does back those who honor their vows.

Marriage has a purpose! This God-designed relationship resembles the relationship between Christ and His Church. This love story was not void of issues; neither was it a seamless, easy thing to do; however, He gave His life for it! That type of display of selfless and sacrificial love goes beyond condition and comprehension.

I don't know if any couple has ever reached that level of unconditional and sacrificial kind of love. However, when couples work toward that level of love, they resemble Christ. Anything that looks like Christ also makes them a target for the enemy. Once the enemy sees Christ's reflection in anything, the attacks and war are on.

YIELD NOT TO TEMPTATION

We cannot afford to be naive to the tactics of the devil. If we are honest, we are aware of the tactics, the weapons formed, the temptations, and the plight, yet we still choose according to the nature of our flesh. Some people who engage in this poor behavior may believe that it is harmless. It may be a game to them or not that big of a deal.

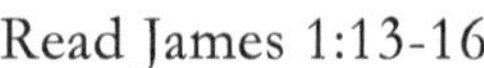
Read James 1:13-16

In verses 13-14, Name the tempter?

After desire conceives in verse 15, it gives birth to what?

When sin is full-grown, it gives birth to what?

Imagine if every sin came to you in "full-grown" form. What if the man or woman you found enticing said to you, "In the end, I will give you a sexually transmitted disease. I will be a crazy baby mama. I will blackmail you for money. If you try to end this, I will confront your spouse with pictures. I will stalk you, or if you make me upset, I will post all of your indiscretions on social media." These are not far-fetched scenarios in various possible outcomes.

We all know how the story ends! There are no happy endings when you choose to sin. In this flesh dwells no good thing, and the heart is deceitful; who can know it. Temptation without the proper perspective will make you believe you can win at a game engineered for you to lose.

This old playbook is why the devil is successful in entering marriages. It's through these common areas of attack. The bible even talks about there being nothing new under the sun. If we understand this statement, we must know that there is a commonality even with temptation.

Discussion Questions:

How do you define temptation?

Give examples of what temptation can look like in a marriage.

When's the last time you intentionally hid/concealed something from your spouse?

Temptations will come, disagreements will happen, and contrasting perspectives can lead to arguments. These issues cause serious breakdowns in marriages and make it easy for the enemy to destroy them. Often, we make the mistake of trying to fill God-voids with unhealthy things and people. They manifest in addictions, substance misuse and abuse, and significant character flaws.

Most people who experience hurtful things in their past allow those experiences to shape how they treat others. Whether married or not, we have all heard horror stories of spouses who do not make clean breaks with old relationships, spouses with addictions, spouses with unresolved traumas from their past, spouses who hold on to offenses, or spouses who lie and deceive. These issues are some of many that occur in a marital relationship.

These unresolved issues create the cycle and pattern of hurt. I am pretty sure you have heard the phrase "Hurt people, hurt people." When it comes to marriage, spouses often use temptations as opportunities to hurt their spouses. Acting on temptations only adds to the problem. It then creates a domino effect of issues and begins to chip away at the foundation of marriage.

Can any of this be avoided? Absolutely! However, I believe the solution begins with transparency and openness during disagreements. If we tip-toe around issues, then it creates the opportunity for temptation.

TELL THE TRUTH

Discussion Questions:

Do you believe it helps or hurts a relationship when you withhold honesty for the sake of peace?

Do you believe being honest with your spouse will bring you closer or push you further apart? Explain your answer.

Why is telling the truth difficult for so many people? Most couples think that concealing some things is easily manageable until it's not! I have seen far too many couples' not be honest with one another. Most of the time to keep the peace; however, when you do not tell the truth, it leaves a foot in the door for the enemy to begin planting seeds of resentment and contempt. Not telling the truth can manifest in subtle ways. It shows up in thoughts and comparisons of your spouse with ex's, resurfacing of previous sexual partners, or allowing imaginations to frame your reality. When these things happen, it is better to be honest with your spouse rather than concealing the truth.

Being honest takes a certain level of vulnerability, not only with your spouse; but with yourself. Telling the truth in love brings a level of transparency and accountability. Sometimes the truth hurts. It does not always make us feel great but is necessary for growth. The bible says it best; when you know the truth, it will set you free! However, when you choose to hide things from your spouse, it is like feeding a monster in the dark.

When you feed these desires, you are unaware of just how big the monster gets. It may seem small to a spouse that entertains past relationships with no proper closure. It may be no big deal to feed sexual appetites with someone other than a spouse. Others even believe it doesn't matter if they develop intimacy with someone other than their spouse. Then someone turns the light on in the situation! Once that happens, the little doorway you allowed this monstrous desire to enter becomes too small to get them out and you end up destroying the walls of your heart for freedom.

A person that enters a marriage relationship with honesty issues finds themselves in this predicament often. They believe they can handle it and "start fresh" and quickly find out it is not that easy. Many spouses find themselves in an uphill battle. Nonetheless, couples looking to move past this error must make it a point, never to feed the monster again!

Discussion Questions:

Can you name any problems/desires you thought you would manage better or absolve through marriage?

When's the last time you have hidden or concealed something from your spouse? What were the effects once revealed?

Is it easy to be honest or transparent with your spouse?

God

"In the beginning" These are the first three words in the bible and should be where God is in any marital relationship- in the beginning. We often gloss over this foundational principle in our dating relationships. We walk on eggshells because we do not want to lose a potential lifelong partner. However, we need God, both as individuals and as a couple. He should be the place from which our mind, heart, and spirit flow.

As believers, we recognize marriage as the first institution God made. He made man first but soon discovered it was not good for him to be alone. He made a helper suitable for him. From the beginning of the bible, we find the relationship between man and woman. In the bible, it talks about Eve being a helper. It does not go into extensive details of the responsibilities of everyone, but they worked with one another.

It was by design that God put man and woman together. He gave them instructions and directives. It was their purpose to be fruitful and multiply. God's instructions never changed, whether they were in the garden or not. No matter the circumstance, God intended that husband and wife work together.

Discussion Question

Do gender roles play into what a "Helper" should be inside of your marriage?

Marriage should resemble Christ's love for the church. We know that Christ loved His bride so much that He gave his life for her. He redeemed her and washed her with the water of the word. That means he cared for her and especially honored her. However, if we are honest, we see very few married couples live this out. Some of us are not even willing to give up our convenience, let alone our life! Today this type of sacrifice is an aspiration for most marriages, not a standard requirement. With this idealism and no application, we lose a lot of the value in marriage.

Discussion Questions:

Wives, what does your husband "laying down" his life look like for you?

Husbands, do you feel it is fair to have the majority of the responsibility to care for and sacrifice for your wife?

Bringing it relevant today, husbands and wives are a collaborative partnership. Whether couples work in different professions or have individual goals and dreams, they should share the responsibility of being helpers, fruitful, and multiplying. When done, it reflects God's original intent and purpose for marriage.

Discussion Questions:

In what areas of your marriage and life have you seen fruitfulness with your spouse? Has anything multiplied?

It is hard to have a healthy relationship with your spouse if you don't have one with God. -Selah. God fills in the gaps that our spouse cannot. God is willing and able to be there for us. This fundamental principle is why we need Him! Giving God priority softens the blow of disappointment when our spouse falls short.

As believers, we need God's help to build a strong marriage. We need God's direction if we desire to fulfill His purpose in it. He becomes the solid foundation on which to build. However, when we choose to value things, not God, we are bound to end up with broken pieces.

God will allow life to expose faulty foundations at some point in our marriage. When we marry for superficial things like sex, money, or looks, we will suffer the consequences of that decision. It reminds me of the fig tree Jesus approached when hungry. It looked great to the eye, but upon closer examination, Jesus found no fruit.

Another example found in Matthew 7:24-27 talks about two houses. One built on a rock and one on the sand. When the flood, wind, and storm came, the house built on sand (superficial things) fell, but the one built on the rock (solid foundation) did not.

Couples who marry for superficial things eventually find out that sex will not solve issues of the heart. Money cannot bribe death, and being sexy will not pay the mortgage. With the wrong foundation, marriages collapse, and we end up with broken pieces.

So, what are the makings of a good foundation? The word of God, which is immutable, and the fruits of the Holy Spirit, which God grows through our experiences! As married couples, we should reflect God's virtue, character, and image.

Discussion Questions:

Take a moment to reflect on the attributes of God. Then choose one that you want to build your marital foundation on.

Choose at least three fruits of the spirit that you would like to see more of in your spouse and why.

Choose one fruit you want to exhibit more to your spouse and why.

The character of God is the best example of how we should live and show up for ourselves and our spouse'. However, things can get out of whack when striving to be more like Christ becomes unilateral. All too often, one spouse shows these characteristics while the other spouse does not. One spouse gives and gives, and the other takes and takes. In other cases, both people possess godly qualities but don't put them into practice. All of these situations are commonplace. When both couples are not putting in the effort, it creates an imbalance between the two. Then frustration and burnout occur.

Just imagine for a second what your marriage would look like if both you and your spouse gave equal consideration, virtue, character, love, and trust to one another all the time. You both would be reflecting a closer image of God to each other. Your understanding of one another would increase while disagreements decrease. However, our culture thrives off of a selfish and individualistic mentality. Many of us are guilty of selfishness because it makes us happy. On the other hand, when it comes to Kingdom principles of serving others-not ourselves, we'd prefer to leave God out of it. When we silence the voice of God, we put our marriages at risk, whether intentionally or not.

I believe one of the most considerable charges God gives us as husband and wife is to see our spouse the way HE sees them! It's difficult to appreciate who we have married until we can see them through the lens of God. As believers, God is our creator. He sees all of us and yet loves us unconditionally. God knows our spouse better than we do! He sees their flaws and their strengths. When you and your spouse run into a problem, be sure to go to God first!

This day in time, it is easier to put God on the back burner and call for Holy Help when we mess things up. We use God as a last resort when we feel we cannot handle things on our own. We can unintentionally put God-sized pressures on our spouses that they are ill-equipped to handle. Once we realize that we need God in our marriage, it is often too late.

When both spouses do not prioritize God in marriage, it causes a constant struggle, and eventually, one or both spouses give up. However, when couples choose to cast their cares on God, strengthen their relationship with Him, and lean on Him, it will inevitably bring them closer together.

In conclusion, God must be at the center of your marriage. If you cannot depend on God to help you through those tough times, you will end up hurting yourself and your spouse. That is why a personal relationship with God is one area you should not compromise. When God is in it, He can change the heart and mind of your spouse. God is full of grace! He created us to share that same grace in our marriage and with our spouses.

Reflection

Take a moment and reflect on how going to God first with everything will help you in your marriage?

Grace

Grace- the "G" word nobody likes to utilize. Isn't it amazing how most people want to receive grace in abundance but ration it out to others? To me, grace is the second biggest "G" word in marriage under God. Grace has several definitions, but I want to focus on; showing kindness to someone inconsiderate of you. Man, this one can be tough! A spouse who is unforgiving and rigid in their thoughts finds it hard to be gracious to their spouse. Grace, if abused, can also be a hindrance to growth and accountability! A spouse can have their graciousness work against them if they do not urge accountability for inappropriate behavior. If not careful, we can end up in disastrous situations either way.

I think of grace as a tightrope. It's easy in theory, like walking a tape line stuck to the floor, but when ascended into the air on nothing but a wire, it becomes a different dynamic.

Many couples fall off this metaphorical tightrope because it is tight! You either find the balance or fail miserably. However, take heart because you possess the ability to display the attribute of grace to your spouses. As we walk this line of grace, God becomes the balancing pole. When we hold onto Him, He helps us keep our balance. As we master this attribute of grace, our spouses are blessed. It also allows us to evolve in areas that have been problematic in our marriage.

Discussion Questions:

In what areas could you show more grace to your spouse? Talk with them about it.

In what areas do you need more grace from your spouse? Explain.

Grace can serve as an intervention while being justified. This one is unique to those who are followers of Christ. It reminds me of the scripture Romans 5:8 "While we were yet sinners Christ died for us." It takes the Holy Ghost to keep from retaliating against a spouse who has wronged you. It's worse if it was done intentionally with no conviction, remorse and is a repeated pattern. Being able to pray for your spouse during those times of blatant offense is not for the faint of heart.

When placed in these situations, grace becomes the place where you and God partner together. Choosing to pray for your spouse while they are in sinful behavior creates an atmosphere of graciousness. Grace makes you die to yourself. You may not be on a literal cross, but your flesh dies every time you choose to show grace.

Another word used to describe grace is intercession. Romans 8:34 talks about Jesus sitting at the right hand of God, interceding for us. We are intercessors for our spouses. If you ever experience betrayal, lies, or manipulation from your spouse, it can be hard to pray for them. However, shift your focus to God, not to your spouse. He will straighten the crooked path and honor the righteousness of the spouse who surrendered the situation to Him.

Take time to reflect on what grace looks like in these painful circumstances (cheating, lying, infidelity, betrayal, etc.). Maybe you have experienced this, or it's your current situation. Take time to talk with your spouse about how grace can help in these instances.

Grace can be a beautiful gift to marriage. It creates a barrier of protection and minimizes the impact of bad decisions. If we struggle to give grace or feel lost in grace, always ask God for wisdom. As couples go through marriage, understanding grace as a currency of love permits everyone to grow and become the best version of themselves. It is my prayer that grace is the currency of unconditional love and not a transactional bid for control. -Selah.

MERCY

Like grace, mercy is something everyone wants to receive in abundance but is unwilling to give. Mercy is the metaphorical "Achilles heel" of the human condition. Everyone wants mercy when they are the offender but are merciless when offended. Having no mercy can be especially dangerous in marriage! If you or your spouse are grudge holders or revenge seekers, this will quicken the erosion of your marital foundation. Without mercy, couples get into a vicious cycle. It usually consists of living in the past and upping each other in the game of pain. Mercilessness shows up in marriage through emotional isolation, silent treatment, and infidelity.

Our culture categorizes mercy as a flaw of weak and ineffective people. Our culture believes that we diminish our worth when we show mercy. People who show mercy are considered feeble, a doormat, a pushover, and one who compromises, but that's the world's view. In the Kingdom of God, mercy is an attribute of the strong! It is part of the beatitudes or beautiful attitudes. The bible says blessed are the merciful because they will obtain mercy.

Merciless people wear the mask of being "tough" or someone who "doesn't take crap." They mock those who practice mercy. It often shows up in conversations like this "Why are you allowing _______ to walk all over you?" "Girl, you don't deserve that." or "You don't need to put up with her crap!" or "I would do to him/her what he/she did to you" or my favorite "You better than me; because it wouldn't be me.......” Merciless people display these ideas like a badge of honor. These opinions state the facts but do not reveal the truth. We can be accurate and still in error. Let that sit for a minute. The world and culture we live in rely on facts and often abandon the truth. The fact is people are human. They make mistakes, but the truth is we all do! We all tend to be that way in some area of our life. Just because we struggle in different ways does not give us the right to be merciless.

Mercy takes spiritual strength and fortitude. It also takes self-control and a solid foundation to stand. Mercy extends the life of a marital relationship and is the ultimate two-way street. When we show mercy to our spouse, we see past the actions and search for the intentions.

Because we are all flawed human beings, our first "go-to" weapon shouldn't be to attack when we can show mercy. We have emotional reflexes that are often triggered by painful or hurtful experiences from our past. Learning to control our emotional response, or as I call it, the knee-jerk reaction takes time and patience. Our response to a hurtful moment shouldn’t be to hurt the other person. When we allow our emotions to drive our decisions, we can jeopardize our marriage. As you decide to do things differently and position yourself to give mercy, you will find that mercy can abound, even in painful parts of marriage.

Positioning yourself in such a way to give mercy can disarm potential breakdowns within your marriage. I will be the first to admit it is not easy! It takes overriding the fleshly desire to pounce- and choosing to answer in gentleness and love.

I would be lying to you if I said showing mercy will immediately change the situation or end the argument. It's something you have to work on! The more you develop and strengthen the spiritual muscle called mercy, the more tenderness you receive from your spouse.

Mercy cannot exist without forgiveness. These two attributes are fused. Without one, the other is impossible to achieve. A characteristic of merciless people is unforgiveness. Merciless people struggle with forgiving others. The biggest recipient of their unforgiveness is themselves. It destroys people from within.

In a marriage, if you have a spouse who has trouble forgiving, usually they have not forgiven themselves for something in their own life. It can manifest itself in judgmental thoughts, attitudes, behaviors, and beliefs towards themselves and others. It also shows up as self-deflection or lack of self-awareness in any situation. A merciless spouse may have an issue with admitting their faults and have an inherent need to be right! If you do not heal these areas within yourself, your spouse becomes the recipient of your rage and absorbs most of the misguided emotions of your mercilessness.

One thing that helped me show mercy in marriage was my relationship with God. The bible tells us that the Lord is rich in mercy. HE had compassion and pity for me when I was wrong. Lord knows I have been the recipient of God's mercy. Mercy is showing kindness and compassion for someone when they have wronged you.

If you ever want to stop merciless behavior, ask yourself this question. "How many times has God shown me mercy when I deserved punishment?" It should bring conviction to a heart ready to receive.

I love that the bible says God is rich in mercy. In other words, God has enough mercy to give to everyone all the time with plenty in stockpile!!! We, as individuals, go bankrupt so quickly with mercy. We show just how deficient we are by phrases we coin-like "3 strikes you're out" or "fool me once, shame on you, fool me twice, shame on me." This thinking becomes embedded into our thoughts and eventually spills over into our marriage.

The bottom line is this! We need mercy if we want our marriages to last. It can be a hard-proverbial pill to swallow but don't regurgitate it or let it get stuck in transit. Wash it down with the water of the word of God through prayer, fasting, and supplication. Once it begins to work its way through your marriage, you will see the difference in your spouse's attitude, reactions, and heart. Be ready to receive that same mercy you extend as well.

Discussion Questions:

In what areas can you show your spouse mercy?

Do you struggle with unforgiveness? Why? If not, why?

How do you think applying the principle of mercy in your marriage can bring you and your spouse closer together?

Where We Go Wrong

With marriage come disagreements. Disagreements are often a difference in perspectives. If not handled correctly, disagreements become the weapons by which we harm our spouse and ourselves. Our words become lethal weapons that we use to tear each other down. It is the only strategy in the enemy's arsenal that does not involve him directly.

Disagreements cause friction between spouses and breakdowns in communication. It contaminates healthy expressions and keeps couples from resolving their issues. As a result, unforgiveness, anger, and isolation creep in. Breakdowns in communication breeds resentment. Then pride becomes the incubator that multiplies all the bad-infectious behaviors. Soon enough, talks about separation or divorce are on the table.

Most couples give up in the throes of building or rebuilding because things get messy. Just think about a construction site. A house does not magically appear without any disruptions. There is a process that happens. Understanding there will be messy moments will keep you from quitting for the greater good of marriage. Don't allow the temporary disappointments to ruin the finished work.

-Wisdom Lesson -

Before you get mad, blow up, storm out, or sin, ask yourself what blessing or promise is waiting on the other side of this? If you take inventory, you will notice a correlation between the problem and the promise given. Therefore, it is so important not to miss these sacred moments to grow and heal.

Discussion Question

What does the spirit of agreement look like inside your household?

Discussion Question

What is a deal-breaker for you inside of your marital relationship? Should deal breakers exist within a marriage?

WORTH FIGHTING FOR

Most people have a "deal-breaker" scenario for leaving their spouse. These deal breakers are different for everyone. Nevertheless, when the trust is gone because someone crossed the line, the reasons to stay become few.

A couple that chooses to move forward within marriage after a violation of any kind faces an uphill battle. Every betrayal inside of marriage takes a toll on both spouses. However, if you both agree to continue in your marriage, there is a possibility for growth, personal development, and healing.

All married couples will go through growing pains. Allowing space for growth does not come without error or correction. Most people believe that violations early in marriage are a testament to future behaviors. Although this is a possibility, we cannot say that the way marriages begin will be how they continue or end. If you believe in the greater good of your spouse, then your marriage is worth the fight! At some point, you are going to have to be willing to contend for your marital relationship.

Discussion Question

Do you believe your marriage is worth fighting for? Why or why not?

We are one

Becoming one with your spouse sounds so beautiful when standing at the altar. However, -if we are honest, most of us take that 'becoming one" line at face value for having sex with our spouse and enjoying it without conviction. However, becoming one with your spouse is so much more than "guilt-free" sex. Becoming one requires sacrifice, laying down your life, and putting your needs after your spouse.

Becoming one does not mean you lose your individuality or identity. Becoming one means choosing to work together in every aspect of each individual's life. It simply means you choose to consider someone else before yourself. It is a difficult task for people who are committed to their happiness.

Often, couples do not realize that unresolved issues are the first weak spots attacked when becoming "one" with their spouse. It often shows itself in many different forms. It may look like the spouse that is typically very passive and easy going, beginning to assert themselves in a way that you may not have seen before. It could be a noticeable disconnect of attention, feelings, and emotions that you previously experienced from your spouse. No matter the circumstance, you can't delegate issues to one spouse. Even if this is the case, at the end of the day you and your spouse are one. Selfishness and self-centeredness cannot coexist in marriage because they are in total opposition to unity and oneness! Until couples understand this principle, issues will remain unresolved.

UNRESOLVED ISSUES

Most married couples don't see the connection between their marital dysfunctions and their household experiences growing up. Whether positive or negative, these expectations influence the way we handle our spouses. It is a critical point in marriage because most people are unwilling to confront painful experiences from their past. Often this is where couples go wrong. If you ever said "I will never..." followed by any statement, this is considered an inner vow. God has a way of confronting all the destructive patterns and judgments we make about ourselves and others. Making inner vows to never be or do something from our past is a sure way to have it come full circle. These conscious decisions confront many people in marital relationships.

The darkness we may have witnessed in other relationships during critical moments of development shapes our views. These experiences tend to show up at the most inopportune times and usually with our spouse. These observations permeate into marital relationships. It shapes our expectations of our spouses and becomes the make or break of the marriage. Without the help of God, these experiences swallow up the joy and beauty of growth we can achieve in marriage.

Let me break it down for you. Let's say you watched your father cheat on your mother for most of your childhood. You saw the arguments and the tears and frustration of your mother. You knew that she loved your father, but he just didn't care to change that particular behavior. When you watched how she stayed and took the hurt, you made an inner vow to yourself. "I'll never put up with this crap from a man" or "I'll never do to another woman what my father did to my mom." These statements are typical responses when watching dysfunctional relationships.

Fast forward some years later, now you are in your relationship or marriage, and low and behold, these same patterns show up. It typically goes one of two ways. The thought of the pattern repeating is repulsive enough for you to throw in the towel and quit. Or you find yourself in a cyclical trend that mirrors what you said you didn't want to become. Both options leave couples feeling hurt, trapped, in shame, and like failures. But I would like to introduce a third option! What if you dare to evolve within the relationship? Taking the focus off all the wrong things your spouse was doing or pressing pause on the repeated cycle. What if you turned it over to God? This option is the one that gets the least attention in a world that feeds on ego, selfishness, and self-gratification.

Now I am not saying that this road less traveled will be easy because it's not. However, this option is the most freeing of any outcomes. It takes the control away from you and places it in God's capable hands! Relinquishing your control is a form of trust and submission to God. He honors your sacrifice and will work on your behalf. The question then becomes, are you strong enough to let go and let God!

Letting go does not mean ending your marriage. What it does mean is opening your hand and loosening your grip on your expectations for your spouse. It can mean separation for a season; it could mean breaking the cycle by doing something different. Today, we have no problem saying "bye-bye" to "toxic" people. But that's not always the answer. Running from everything never solves anything.

I noticed that many couples lost their fortitude. When marriage doesn't make them feel good or happy, they will cut it off or write it off like bad debt. Many couples tend to quit. Therefore, divorce rates have skyrocketed. Somewhere down the line, people believed that getting rid of the person gets rid of the problem. However, when couples don't do their work, they will see it in the next relationship they engage.

Marriage, at its best, is an evolution of two individuals becoming who God intended for them to be while together. Marriage at its worst is using someone out of self-serving ambitions or bad intentions with no regard for their future.

Discussion Questions

Can you name a time when you felt like calling it quits in your marriage?

Now that you have identified the incident that pushed you to the edge, what made you stay?

Another derailment of marriage is hearing but not actively listening to your spouse. Although most will not admit it, we tend to listen to what we want or think; rather than hear the heart and spirit of our spouse. We get caught up in words and miss the place from which it comes. Communication affects how we feel about our spouse. When a communication breakdown occurs, it creates a void. If not filled, that void becomes the access point for someone else. No wonder the bible says to make sure the sun does not go down on your wrath.

Communication is a valuable tool that is needed to make the journey of life together. Your words frame your martial space. Choosing your words can bring life or death to your marriage. Conversations with your spouse can define or destroy your marriage. Most couples make the mistake of using their words as weapons against one another. It is so much easier to blame each other when arguments come rather than listening to gain understanding. Listening takes the capacity to see things from your spouse's point of view. It takes openness, compassion, and vulnerability. Listening gives your spouse a safe space in which to share their feelings, emotions, and experiences with you. When communication with your spouse no longer feels like a safe space but a chore, then it's time for some intervention!

Making it Through Tough Times

Marriage is hard work! If it were easy, we all would desire it and be successful at it. The fact of the matter is it takes depth and capacity to deal with someone outside of your own beliefs, behaviors, and ideas. Therefore, sharing common values is a widely accepted prerequisite for marital commitments.

Even with all the boxes checked, having similarities and compatibility, there are many differences between you and your spouse. As much as couples can agree on things, there are still plenty of things to disagree on as well. Even through disagreements, both spouses have to decide to keep moving forward like time. Think of marriage like a clock.

In this analogy, the three hands on the clock would be you, your spouse, and how you two work together. Each gear works simultaneously and autonomously to complete the work, and as a result, it accurately reflects the time. Think of the numbers as God because the purpose and intent never change. The marriage clock is there for others to see and offer accuracy and dependability. When all the parts work together, it should achieve a godly marriage. If marriage is successful, it will help other couples to see things in time. A marriage in-tune is accurate, trustworthy, and dependable.

If you have been married for some years, I can bet there are times your marital clock gears have grinned, stopped, malfunctioned, or downright broke. Thank God that you don't have to stay in that condition. It is normal to any marital relationship. This is why it is good to have someone look at the damage and give you an assessment of the problem. Thank God for therapists! They help to mediate and navigate the problems between you and your spouse. Before you run from the topic of therapy, consider them as a resource in marriage. They are trained to help couples unpack suppressed and unresolved issues. Therapists are a sounding board for both you and your spouse. If your spouse suggests this alternative, don't run or shut them down. You never know how therapy can help if you never try it.

No matter how deeply you desire a peaceful and loving life with your spouse, conflicts will arise, and compromises are necessary. When couples choose to be stubborn or inflexible, they run the battery life out of their marital clock. The gridlock of ideas and destructive behaviors pull at the power of your marriage, and eventually, the clock will stop.

Sometimes in marriage, compromise is hard, especially if you and your spouse feel very strongly about your convictions. I love the saying, "pick and choose your battles." It is a wise strategy that can help you to create a baseline for conflict resolution. You have to decide whether or not it's worth the energy. You should ask yourself these two questions before confronting your spouse with anything.

Question 1: Is this going to cause friction in our household?

Question 2: If so, am I ready to compromise if possible?

Exercise Some clichés we hear are words of wisdom. Over time they have lost their power because we heard it so much. List some of the clichés you hear around marriage and compromise.

If we are not careful, we can spend a lot of time and energy arguing over frivolous things.

Exercise: Can you recall a time where you and your spouse argued over something minuscule? What was it, and how long did the argument last?

If we search the scriptures on how we conduct ourselves during a disagreement, many of us would be guilty of mismanagement of the situation and our emotions. Take a few moments to see what scripture comes to mind when you talk about resolution.

Ephesians 4:29
Let no unwholesome word proceed from your mouth, but only such a word as is good for edification according to the need of the moment; so that it will give grace to those who hear.

1 Peter 3:8-11
To sum up, all of you be harmonious, sympathetic, brotherly, kindhearted, and humble in spirit; not returning evil for evil or insult for insult, but giving a blessing instead; for you were called for the very purpose that you might inherit a blessing.

Proverbs 15:1
A gentle answer turns away wrath, but a harsh word stirs up anger.

Matthew 5:9
"Blessed are the peacemakers, for they shall be called sons of God.

Colossians 3:13
bearing with one another, and forgiving each other, whoever has a complaint against anyone; just as the Lord forgave you, so also should you.

Discussion Questions

Which of these scriptures resonates with you? Which one convicts you? How can scriptures like these come in handy during any conflict?

When we spend too much time arguing over little things, we are likely to mishandle the big stuff when it comes. For example, if you spend more than 5 minutes over the tissue roll being over, not under, then chances are it's not about the tissue. It is something more than that. These arguments often happen because of the residue of unfinished business.

Exercise: Can you recall a time you and your spouse argued over something minuscule? Was there another issue you were afraid to confront at that time? Talk it out with your spouse.

Sometimes we don't have the language to express what we want or need from our spouse. Translating our emotions to language is a skill that takes work to develop and requires a level of vulnerability. The inability to express clearly what our spirit is feeling can manifest itself in one or both spouses lashing out. It is especially true when it comes to painful situations.

Often, we don't deal with or heal the root of our issues. However, we become masters at making our spouses feel the wrath of our emotions through our words. It's much easier to lash out and blame our spouses rather than take a moment to form, develop, and fruitfully express ourselves. Dealing with our issues will help us to make it through tough times.

In order to make it through the tough times and seasons of marriage, we must be willing to die to "self" for a season. It is an essential mindset when it comes to surviving the rough times in marital relationships. Once we are resolved in our decision to make it work, we give our marriages a fighting chance!

The Conclusion

Without God, grace, and mercy, it is impossible to have a healthy, fruitful, and successful marriage. When we put all these principles in motion, we have the blueprint for a better relationship. As I mentioned above, take inventory of what changes need to occur in your marriage and ask God for wisdom. I pray that couples will take these principles to build and create a marriage relationship they enjoy. I also pray for reconciliation and restoration in toxic marriages. I also pray that couples in crisis get unstuck from the same narrative and muster the courage to change their situations. Always remember, with God, all things are possible!

On the next page I put together a pledge to one another. I believe in speaking well over your marriage and your spouse. I will give you the format to fill in according to your needs. Once concluded, this will become the blueprint for your survival through tough times. When you and your spouse fill in the blanks, re-write it like a mission statement and place it somewhere where both of you see it. Confess it daily over your marriage, both individually and as a couple.

We pledge to love God first and then one another. We will show our commitment to one another by________________.

When problems arise in our marriage we will
____.

We will show each other grace by
____ and extend mercy in ____.

We will work to produce spiritual fruit for our spouses to eat upon like ____________________________________, knowing that God is________________________________.

We ask for wisdom in ________________________________ and when in conflict we commit to resolve it quickly using the strategies we gained in this workbook.

We choose to speak life over our marriage, especially in the areas of ______________________________________We ask for God's blessing and will over all these things. Amen!

Thank you so much for reading my book! I hope this blessed you and causes healing in your relationship!

-Natalie

www.ingramcontent.com/pod-product-compliance
Ingram Content Group UK Ltd.
Pitfield, Milton Keynes, MK11 3LW, UK
UKHW042010190726
13854UKWH00005B/2234